KV-658-686

Successful
Presentations

FRANCIS BERGIN

DIRECTOR BOOKS

PUBLISHED IN ASSOCIATION WITH THE INSTITUTE OF DIRECTORS

First published 1995 by
Director Books
an imprint of Fitzwilliam Publishing Limited
Campus 400, Maylands Avenue
Hemel Hempstead
Hertfordshire, HP2 7EZ
A division of
Simon & Schuster International Group

© Francis Bergin, 1995

All rights reserved. No part of this publication may be reproduced, stored in a retrieval system, or transmitted, in any form, or by any means, electronic, mechanical, photocopying, recording or otherwise, without prior permission, in writing, from the publisher.

The views of the author do not necessarily represent those of the Council of the Institute of Directors

Typeset in 10/13pt Sabon with Franklin Gothic
by Hands Fotoset, Leicester

Illustrations by Maria Staples

Printed and bound in Great Britain by
T. J. Press (Padstow) Ltd.

British Library Cataloguing in Publication Data

A catalogue record for this book is available from the British Library

ISBN: 0-13-434143-0

2 3 4 5   99 98 97 96

Contents

Preface   vii

1 Introduction   1
2 The purpose   5
3 Know your audience   11
4 Preparation and notes   19
5 Delivery   29
6 Body language   35
7 Getting results   41
8 Visual aids   49
9 Dealing with nervousness   57
10 Dealing with questions and objections   63
11 The media interview   71
12 After Dinner speaking   77
13 Special occasions   81
14 The main pitfalls   89

Index   91

Preface

This short book is based on experience gained during over twenty-five years of presenting to groups of as few as four and as many as six thousand! It also draws on observations made while training many hundreds of directors and senior managers at The Centre for Director Development and elsewhere. And it draws too on listening to countless presentations both good and bad, the ratio of these being around 1:8!

The most frequently asked questions on courses are dealt with as are the anxieties most often expressed by those who find business presentations one of their least welcome tasks – and that's probably a majority of business men and women.

It is *not* designed as a 'text book on presentations'. I don't believe presentational skills can be taught solely from a text book to people you've never even met. But the book *is* designed to give, in the minimum amount of time, some very helpful reminders to those of us who lecture, present and speak to audiences we already know and to audiences to whom we may be speaking for the first time.

Nor is it exhaustive: only the most important points are covered as the book is intended for busy directors and executives whose time for reading detailed tomes is all too limited. And at the end of each chapter there's a helpful checklist highlighting the most important 'do's' and 'don'ts' from the chapter itself.

Please be assured that if you adhere to the simple guidelines in the pages which follow you will make an excellent impression on those to whom you speak and your chances of achieving your objectives will be greatly enhanced.

CHAPTER ONE

Introduction

Blessed are they who have nothing to say and cannot be
persuaded to say it.

JAMES RUSSELL LOWELL

Everyone wants to be able to speak confidently to any group of
people, whether large or small. Most people think the ability to do
this is unique. It is not. If you follow a set of commonsense rules
you will become effective in a reasonably short time. But there are
no short cuts. You must follow the basic rules, and this book confines
itself to these.

Today, businessmen and businesswomen present far more often
than was the case even ten or fifteen years ago. For example, firms
of solicitors, accountants, surveyors and consultants all present on
a regular basis in a very competitive environment. The days of
building up a business simply from contacts on the golf course have
long since gone. So, being able to present well is a skill we all need
nowadays. Since I first began training in this area over twenty-five
years ago there has been a noticeable improvement in the way people
present, which means (unfortunately for you!) that you are likely
to be compared to fairly competent people.

On being asked to make a presentation, many of us become
nervous and diffident. We become defensive. The language we use
seems impersonal and stilted and we appear unapproachable and
ill at ease. One of the keys to avoiding these pitfalls is to realise

that the word *present* means 'to bring, to offer or to make a gift to'. If we approach the exercise from this standpoint we'll think of our listeners more than of ourselves and in many ways presenting will become enjoyable, even, at times, fun!

The reason this book is so confined is twofold. First, you probably don't have nearly enough time to read as much as you would like. Second, we're all unique, and if you try to put yourself into some kind of straitjacket of techniques it will never work. Because you are unique it is important that you present as much as possible in your own natural style. If you work and work on all kinds of complicated techniques involving elocution, oratory and so on, you'll end up forgetting what you are really trying to say. And you'll also become a kind of actor: actors need techniques in order to become someone else – you don't.

Over the years I've seen people make every conceivable mistake in their presentations and I've made my fair share – indeed, more than my fair share – of mistakes too. But I've learned from theirs, and mine; and this short book will help you avoid giving the kind of poor presentation where everyone, including you, is slightly embarrassed when you've finished speaking, and no one knows quite what to do or say next.

Many surveys have been conducted, particularly in the USA, which show that, among all the skills learned by senior businessmen, the ability to communicate effectively is always at, or near, the top.

The most important principle in business presentations/public speaking (and from here on we'll refer to business presentations/ public speaking/lecturing and so on, as 'speaking') is that *you thoroughly prepare every time you speak*. There are no short cuts to this principle. If you think there must be some way of speaking effectively without preparing, don't bother to read any further! And anyone who tells you there is some magic formula doesn't know his arm from his elbow in this important area.

CHAPTER TWO

The purpose

If you aim at nothing you're sure to hit it.

ANON

Put briefly, the aims and objectives of effective speaking in business are: *to know what to say, when to say it and how to say it.*

I know you don't live in an ideal world and time is always at a premium but the more time you spend in preparation the more effective your speech will be. As a general rule you should spend about one hour in preparation for every five minutes of speaking, up to a maximum of five or six hours after which you can probably speak non-stop for hours on any topic which takes your fancy! That's not to suggest that you lock yourself away for hours at a time. By 'preparation' I mean thinking about the subject, reading material from various sources, jotting down items from your experience, chatting to colleagues and others about the subject and then writing your notes, at least in outline form.

Within this process of preparation your most vital element is your Specific Purpose Statement (SPS). I prefer to put it like this rather than say Statement of Objectives for the simple reason that it sounds crisper. You must ask yourself what *precisely* it is that you are trying to achieve. There must be no area of vagueness in your SPS. It's no use saying, 'My SPS is to increase the return on my company's capital employed'. That's everyone's objective all the time. *Precisely how* will your speech help achieve this purpose?

The SPS is paramount. If you don't think that through, or can't agree on what it is with your colleagues in a team presentation, you're finished! The SPS is the purpose, the objective, the aim, the target of your presentation. And you should tell your audience what it is too.

There are several reasons why you might have to speak to a group of people. Among them are the following:

- You may wish simply to inform your audience.
- You may be 'pitching' for business and attempting to get your company's name on a short list.
- You may have to reassure your staff, your customers or your shareholders.
- You may be seeking to change the attitude of your audience.
- You may be asked to speak just to entertain your listeners, as is the case in After Dinner speeches or social occasions.

But for most of us, we probably speak in order to persuade, to get people to understand something and then do it.

Uppermost in your mind, however, must be the overriding aim of 'serving' your audience and being of benefit to them in some way. Otherwise there's really no reason for their listening to you. Every single audience is guided by the WIIFM principle – 'What's in it for me?'

At this stage never mind the 'how' and don't worry about visual aids, etc. Spend enough time to work out your precise SPS. As it says at the beginning of this chapter, 'If you aim at nothing you're sure to hit it' or to put it another way, 'If you don't know where you're going, you'll end up somewhere else!'

In setting out your SPS ask yourself questions like these:

- What can I reasonably expect my audience to do as a result of my speech? Remember that the word 'reasonably' is important here: the SPS must be achievable.

- What can I reasonably expect to change in the beliefs or practices of my audience? Again the word 'reasonably' is basic. You can't expect to change the beliefs of a lifetime in thirty minutes.
- What can I expect to achieve in the limited time available? You will *always* be constrained by time.

In asking, and more importantly, answering these questions you will bring a degree of precision to your thoughts and your speech and you won't set out foolishly to try to achieve the impossible.

Once you have decided on your SPS it will naturally follow throughout the remainder of your presentation that nothing which does *not* support your SPS is said, shown or done. Anything which adds nothing to your SPS must be discharged however attractive or pithy it may appear. By sticking rigidly to your SPS you will avoid the hallmarks of many a poor speech which are:

- Disjointed ideas
- Dislocated thoughts
- Fractured concepts.

So, tedious though it may appear to be, *always* write out your SPS in a single sentence as your first step in preparation.

Public speaking is always a purposeful activity; that purpose in large measure controls what you say and how you say it. All general topics are capable of various interpretations so, if you are asked to speak on a subject by an organisation other than your own, make sure you and they agree on the *precise* nature of the topic *and* their reason for wishing the topic covered. Insist too, politely, that the organisers tell those who are expected to attend your speech, what it is you will be covering and, if the subject is a large one, what particular aspect(s) you'll deal with.

Having reached this stage, the next issue on which you must make up your mind is how you are going to structure what you have to say in order to achieve your SPS. We'll look at that in Chapter 4 under the subject of Preparation but one issue is important at this early stage. And that's the issue of how many points you are going to make (and develop) in order to achieve your SPS. So let's establish right now how people count when they listen to a speech containing point after point. They count One, Two, Three, Four, A Lot, Too Many! As a general rule, therefore, no speech should have more than four main points and preferably just three.

But remember: *everything you say and do and show, from the moment you begin until the moment you conclude, must support your Specific Purpose Statement.*

CHECKLIST

1. *Allow ample time for thorough preparation.* There is no short cut in this area. You cannot possibly give a good presentation if you are ill-prepared.

2. *Write out in longhand your Specific Purpose Statement.* This will help concentrate your mind on the precise objective of the exercise.

3. *Ensure your SPS really is precise.* The crisper this is the more likely you are to achieve your desired goal.

4. *Make sure your Specific Purpose is achievable in the time available.* Indeed, ensure that it's achievable with a few minutes to spare.

5. *Don't say, show or do ANYTHING which does not directly support your SPS.* Chop out ALL extraneous matter.

6. *Limit your main points to three or, at most, four.* People tire easily when listening to others!

CHAPTER THREE

Know your audience

There is perhaps no greater hardship at present inflicted on mankind in civilized and free countries than the necessity of listening to someone else.

ANTHONY TROLLOPE

One of the most common pitfalls for speakers is that they approach a subject from a single point of view: *their own*! After all it's your very own presentation. You have lovingly prepared it. You're in charge, or at least you're the expert on the subject. You have all sorts of information to impart which you have researched carefully. And you are enthusiastic about what you are going to say. *But you forget the audience at your peril.*

It may perhaps seem unusual in a book such as this to talk about *caring* for your audience. But if you don't care it will show. And by caring I mean being concerned enough that you tailor your speech to your listeners. You will not speak in the same terms to women as you will to men. You will not speak in the same language to professionally qualified people as you will to factory workers. It is not that you will – or should – think more highly of one group than another; it's simply that the language you will use, the anecdotes you choose to relate, the examples you give will relate precisely to the type of people to whom you are speaking. You give, in effect, of yourself by tailoring your message to your particular audience.

In the last chapter we looked at the objective. In other words we asked: 'What are we trying to convey?' The very next question we should ask is: 'To whom are we trying to convey it?' To answer this you have to try and get inside the mind of your audience. *All* messages must be delivered from *their* point of view. Presenting a topic from your point of view only will alienate an audience. This applies whether you are speaking within or outside your own particular organisation. So, for example, to begin with that well-worn phrase, 'What I want to tell you about (or talk to you about) today is . . .' means you are on a loser from the word go. Audiences don't want to be told. It's much better to say, 'We'll discuss', or 'We'll explore', or 'You'll discover'.

Within your own company you'll usually know your audience (indeed, you may know them well enough to be able to address one or two or even several by name as you progress through your speech) but if you are speaking to an outside audience find out, or have someone find out for you, the following:

- Is it a mixed audience or all male/female?
- The age group present
- The racial mix
- The occupation/profession of your listeners
- Their job titles and responsibilities
- Their mood and expectations
- How up to date they are
- The levels of prejudice and resistance (if any)
- Their educational level
- How much they already know about the subject
- Their limits of authority
- The number likely to attend.

Almost every piece of information you find out can be used in some way or another to your advantage. But if you pitch your speech at the wrong level you will alienate part or all of your listeners.

One golden rule to observe with all audiences is: *Never underestimate their intelligence and never overestimate their knowledge.*

INTERACTION WITH YOUR AUDIENCE

As far as your interaction with your audience is concerned there are four main areas with which you must be concerned. These fall under the following headings which we'll amplify briefly below:

- Expectation
- Recognition
- Involvement
- Capacity to act.

At the beginning let your audience know what to *expect*. They have to shift their minds into gear to listen to you and don't like sudden jolts or surprises. If listeners are expecting some useful information, they will grasp it much more rapidly when you deliver it than they will if they don't know quite what to *expect*. So tell them the areas you are going to cover and how your talk will be structured but make sure that you *do not deviate from what you tell them*. (Your personal appearance and facial expression have an important bearing on this aspect of interaction. It would obviously be quite inappropriate to appear lighthearted and dressed to match if you are going to deliver a message that's sombre, grave or very serious.)

We all want attention and we all want *recognition*. The 'all' includes our audiences. Therefore, demonstrate clearly by the way you speak to them and handle your subject that you recognise *their* interests, concerns and aspirations. Say things like, 'As many of you managers will have experienced' or 'As I'm sure most of you accountants are all too well aware'. That keeps you from sounding condescending to your audience. And don't talk in abstract terms or concepts that are difficult to visualise or grasp. Pay full attention to your listeners all the time: that's what's meant by *recognition*.

You can *involve* your audience by occasionally asking a rhetorical question. The rhetorical question is designed to get your audience involved in what you are saying. The question encourages them to think up their own answers which makes them concentrate on your message and consider if your answer will match theirs. But make your question *sound* as if it really is a question; then pause, thus giving the audience a few seconds in which to think it through.

You can also *involve* them by asking them to 'recall for a moment the example we used of the US company producing . . .'. Again give them a few seconds to shift their minds into gear and participate, as they mentally recall the point you made earlier. Asking your audience to imagine a particular scenario relevant to your speech is also a useful technique for holding their attention.

And you must also let them know where you are in your speech from time to time if it's any longer than about five minutes. For example, you can say, 'And having covered the European market scene, let's move on to North America'. When you read a book you can go back and check names, dates, items that you may have forgotten or events which have perhaps become a bit of a blur if you haven't looked at it for some time. But you can't do that when listening to a speaker. Your task then as a speaker is to remind your listeners where you've been and where you're at. This technique is called verbal flagging (or verbal paragraphing) and is yet another technique for keeping your listeners *involved*.

Do remember, when you ask an audience to do something, to limit your request to actions which lie within their range of authority or *capacity to act*. You determine the range of authority perhaps through your position within your own company but if your listeners are an outside audience you determine their range of authority through your earlier analysis of the audience, especially through demographic factors. You will, or should, always know the limits of authority when you speak inside your own organisation.

If, incidentally, in order to achieve what you ask, some further facilities must be made available to your listeners, then promise them these too. Don't ever ask too much of your listeners. And when appealing for action, always demonstrate the logic and even the necessity of your request.

And do look at your audience. If looking directly into their eyes is a problem then look at their foreheads or their ears or noses – but look at them. They expect that. If you and I were talking over a drink in the pub you would think it most odd if I never looked you in the eye. Not only would it seem odd but I would seem a distinctly 'shifty character'. Audiences large or small feel exactly the same. And you can't possibly know how your speech is being received – nor make any spontaneous changes – if you're not looking at your listeners.

Finally, you must affect your audience in such a way that: *they* know that *you* know what you're talking about; they *understand* what you have been talking about; and they appreciate that what you have said is real and personal to them in their business lives.

CHECKLIST
---

1. *Approach the subject matter from the audience's viewpoint, not your own.* The question we all have when listening to any presentation is: 'What's in it for me?'

2. *Analyse your audience: every piece of information can be useful.* Try to share their culture as much as possible.

3. *Let them know what to expect from you.* Don't inflict a kind of mental 'whiplash' on your listeners.

4. *Show that you understand their interests and concerns.* The more you identify with them the more they'll identify with you.

5. *Keep them involved throughout.* Stimulate their thinking by asking questions. Let them know where you are in your presentation and what you'll be covering next.

6. *Don't appeal for action beyond their capacity to act.* Pitch your appeal at the right level.

7. *Don't talk down to them.* It's easily done and is usually unintentional.

8. *Look at them.* Look at all of them. Look at all your audience most of the time!

CHAPTER FOUR

Preparation and notes

I find that a great part of the information I have was
acquired by looking up something and finding
something else on the way.

FRANKLIN P. ADAMS

Sometimes the subject of the talk will be chosen for you; on other
occasions you will originate the subject entirely. And it's usually
much easier to talk on your own subject than on one which is
assigned.

BE SPECIFIC

You need to be particularly careful with a subject which is not of
your own choosing in establishing *precisely* what the organisers
want from you, and you also need to be crystal clear that you and
they attach the same meaning to the title of the speech. Unless it is
an After Dinner situation, I try to decline politely invitations to
speak on topics selected by others. I have accepted such invitations
in the past, spoken (brilliantly, of course!) throughout on what *I*
thought the audience were expecting, only to find at the conclusion
of my talk that there was an atmosphere of general surprise and,
in a few instances, disappointment!

BUILDING THE PRESENTATION

Building a presentation is rather like building a house. You build it in stages. Never attempt to write out your speech in just one sitting. The only time that's appropriate is on the rare occasion when you are speaking impromptu.

I recommend that you start with the scattergram approach. Keep a few sheets by your desk or in your pocket and jot down all you know about the subject you're going to address, *having first written down your Specific Purpose Statement*. Add thoughts and ideas immediately they occur to you from day to day. (If you don't get into the habit of adding them *immediately* they come into your mind you'll inevitably forget them – until about an hour or two *after* you've given your speech!) Then over a few days you will begin to have some idea of what you want to say.

You will have several sources from which to draw. All business organisations have internal product descriptions, house journals, newsletters, reports, etc. You may also want to refer to external sources of information such as trade reports, professional journals, Government reports or White Papers, newspaper articles and so on. And then you will also have your own experience and expertise on which to draw. There will be anecdotes, stories, opinions from your own business life which will add freshness and 'punch' to your speech. (From this you will note that to read widely and to keep up to date are very important for someone who speaks regularly.) You should collect the various items you need and keep them in a folder with your notes until you get down to your final preparation.

At this stage you determine your main points. Make sure you meet the objectives of your SPS with these main points. Make sure they are clearly and accurately supported. Try to think of, and answer, any questions which you might expect your listeners to raise as a result of what you are going to say. And ensure your main points are organised in a sequence that leads to a logical and dynamic conclusion. So you delete, change, simplify, rearrange, add, qualify and get it all in shape.

Remember that *all* speeches must have the following three components which ought to be as clear to your listeners as they are to you:

- The introduction
- The body
- The conclusion.

That seems terribly obvious, I know, but sadly you've probably heard many presentations in your business life where you could hardly distinguish between these three, much less understand what the speaker was trying to achieve.

THE INTRODUCTION AND CONCLUSION

The *introduction* to your speech can be difficult but it is also highly important, simply because the minds of your listeners are freshest when you begin and are therefore comparatively easy to impress. But the introduction is far too important to be left to chance and it's far too significant to craft it around some kind of joke or humorous story. You can, however, relate a human interest story, or arouse curiosity, or begin with a specific illustration. You can also ask the audience a question or open with a striking quotation. But I believe, for the kind of audiences senior business men and women will be addressing, the best way to begin is to show how your topic affects their vital interests. Tell them you have the solution to one of their particular problems or, through listening to you, something they desire for the best of motives will come to pass.

I always recommend that *your first and last sentences are written out in full.* And that includes, 'Good morning, Ladies and Gentlemen . . .' Our minds can go blank for just a second or two when we stand up to speak and you must give no impression of not *quite* knowing where you are or what you're supposed to be saying next.

We'll look at the *body* of your speech later, but your *conclusion* is always highly important because what's said last is likely to be

THE HENLEY COLLEGE LIBRARY

remembered longest. Many speakers stop a long time before they finish speaking: they are rather like an airline captain desperately seeking some landing strip and while searching they seem to circle endlessly, to the extreme annoyance of their audience.

You can end by paying the audience a sincere compliment, by appealing for action, by building up to a kind of climax or by using a fitting quotation. But in my view the best way for you to end the type of speech you will normally give in a business context is to summarise what you have said briefly and in the order in which you said it. At this stage do *not* introduce any additional items which did not appear in the body of your speech. If you do, you'll not only confuse your audience but cause them to mistrust you too. You can always re-use what you had in your introduction thereby giving a complete linkage from start to finish.

However, your ending must be graceful. Don't end by saying something like, 'My time is up so I think I'll conclude', or 'I think that's all I have to say on the subject so I'd better stop'!

The summary form of conclusion is best for another reason too. Experts tell us that we forget 50% of what we hear within 24 hours and about 80% of what we hear within 72 hours, so repetition is no bad thing.

One last point: don't keep saying 'finally', and 'in conclusion', and 'to end' and so on. When you say 'finally' mean it, and when you utter that word you are hoist by your own petard because, for your audience, hope springs eternal in the human breast!

YOUR NOTES

Your notes should be written or typed on cards about $9'' \times 7''$ rather than on A4 sheets of paper. We look clumsy when we try to handle large sheets of paper as we speak. Number your cards clearly in the top right-hand corner.

People always ask, 'How many notes should I have?' The correct answer is: as many as make *you* feel comfortable. Some require more than others. But don't be embarrassed because you have to use notes or because your notes are fairly comprehensive. Audiences expect you to have notes: they show you have at least prepared what you are going to say. You should not therefore make any attempt to hide them.

Notes serve four purposes. They:

- Help your mental preparation
- Help you define what is really relevant
- Help you exclude the unnecessary (back to the SPS again!)
- Keep you on course and on time.

Make sure your notes contain words which help. There's no point in writing on your card 'And another thing is . . .', simply because you'll forget what the other thing is!

Just to demonstrate what your notes could look like (using only one card in this example):

Introduction
1. Main point
   (a) Supporting example
   (b) Supporting data
   (c) Supporting experience
2. Main point
   (a) Development
   (b) Supporting statistics
3. Main point

   Appeal for action
   Summary
   Concluding remarks.

Do remember that notes are not a substitute for knowledge. They are simply to remind you of facts you already know.

Your notes are personal to you – no one else is going to see them. Therefore you can write reminders on your notes which will help your delivery. If you have a tendency to speak too quickly (a problem, incidentally, with most inexperienced speakers) write 'Slow down' several times in type large enough to see. Maybe you speak too softly – then just include 'Speak louder' in your notes. These reminders will help keep you on track throughout your speech.

'THE MOTIVATED SEQUENCE'

Many textbooks suggest that business people use what they call 'The motivated sequence presentation'. I heartily agree. It may not be the perfect structure for all occasions but it's certainly appropriate for many speeches. Here's what it looks like and it really needs little explanation:

1. The attention step
2. The need step
3. The satisfaction step
4. The visualisation step
5. The action step.

We gain the *attention* of our listeners at the beginning and then show them what is *needed* or define the problem which *needs* to be solved. We then demonstrate how this need is to be *satisfied*. In other words, we present our solution to their problem. We follow this by helping them *visualise* how our solution will work. Often this can be done by using examples of where it is now satisfactorily working. And we then conclude by showing what *action* needs to be taken, when, and by whom.

The motivated sequence speech is a punchy and logical kind of presentation and works well in a business context despite its rather elaborate title!

As you begin to speak regularly you'll become less dependent on notes but you should never try to do without them altogether. Even if you don't really need them all the time – or even if you feel you need them none of the time – their preparation will force you to be logical in your presentation. You'll often find too that interruptions and distractions occur (not to mention the fact that the mind can sometimes go completely blank), so it's always safe to have them at hand.

REHEARSE

The last stage of your preparation, until you become a very experienced speaker, is to practise the speech exactly as you will deliver it. Stand up at home, in your office, or wherever you wish and give the speech just as you will on the day in question. Don't just read it – speak it. I know that will feel most unnatural but you'll get used to it in time. We can read somewhere around 900 words a minute but for a speech the ideal speed is around 175 words a minute and if you just *read* it in rehearsal you'll have no idea how long it will actually take to speak. Don't go on rehearsing for ever. After about one or two attempts leave it there, otherwise it will become boring to you and if it seems boring to you, just imagine what it will be like for your audience!

Do remember that, for reasons which nobody seems to quite understand, the real presentation will be about 10% longer than the rehearsal. If it isn't, good for you. Your listeners will appreciate your finishing slightly ahead of schedule!

CHECKLIST

1. *Once again, remember to be quite specific in your purpose.* Include only what will clearly support your objective.
2. *Don't try to prepare your speech in just one sitting.* Speeches grow from day to day.
3. *Separate your introduction, body and conclusion.* Make sure these are as clear to your audience as they are to you.

4. *Prepare helpful notes.* They're your notes — no one else will see them — so write on them whatever reminders you need.

5. *Arrange your material (main points, supporting material and transitions) in logical order.* This is what will take most of your preparation time.

6. *Write out your first and last sentences in full.* In this way if, for some inexplicable reason, you get confused your beginning and ending will be crisp and businesslike.

7. *Rehearse at least once.* You must have a grasp of how long it's going to take and that's the point at which you can make adjustments. It's too late when you're standing behind the lectern on the fateful day!

CHAPTER FIVE

Delivery

The nice thing about being a celebrity is that
when you bore people they think it's their fault.

————

HENRY KISSINGER

The less experienced speaker usually encounters a problem the moment he or she stands up to speak. This hinges on the fact that the audience greets a speaker with total silence. If we are chatting as a group in an informal setting there will be nods, smiles, noises and so on which form part of the normal conversational experience. But when we stand before an audience there is no reaction whatever. That can be unnerving. However, it is exactly what is supposed to happen. Therefore, be prepared for this reception. It certainly does *not* mean your audience are hostile: it's simply the normal way in which the average audience responds. They are being attentive and courteous.

Delivery refers to the methods by which you communicate what you have to say to your audience. You deliver your message to people through three channels:

- Verbal
- Vocal
- Visual.

VERBAL

Never use clichés or overworked phrases such as, 'At this moment in time', 'In this day and age', 'At the end of the day', 'The bottom line', 'The jury is still out' and so on. Expressions such as these become stale very quickly and bore audiences half to death.

In quoting any authority, always use the present tense: for example, 'Churchill tells us', 'Socrates reminds us', or 'Shakespeare puts it this way'. This gives immediacy to what you're trying to put across.

And it goes without saying – or should – that your grammar and syntax should be correct. It's always surprised me, while leading courses consisting of well-educated and experienced people, to hear so many mangle the English language unnecessarily. There really is no need for this and when it occurs it doesn't sit well with your audience.

As mentioned earlier, when you speak you should involve your listeners as much as is practicable.

It's important too that you pause at your points of transition. You should remind your audience of the points you've covered and tell them where you're going next; for example, 'Having looked at the use of computer graphs in our industry in the UK, let's now move on to consider their uses in the US.' This tells your audience where they are in the presentation and what to expect over the next few minutes.

VOCAL

As in normal speech, you should have a variety of sentence lengths: a host of long rambling sentences one after another serves only to confound an audience.

In normal conversation our voice varies in sound as we speak.

This helps keep our listeners interested. When we speak to a group, our voice should vary too. Don't try to put on some kind of orator's voice. And don't ever try to model yourself on another speaker: what works well for him or her may not suit your personality one bit. A monotone presentation will send your listeners to sleep – and you too perhaps! Your voice needs to alter throughout in three distinct ways:

- Pitch
- Power
- Pace.

As you would normally, speak louder about the more important issues. Vary the speeds: asides are usually delivered a little faster than the main points of argument or persuasion, but do make sure they can still be heard. Many speakers have the habit of allowing the ends of their sentences to fall away into a quiet whisper. This frustrates an audience who want to hear everything that's said. Indeed, with many speakers their asides can be interesting and often highly amusing.

And we must never forget to articulate clearly, particularly our consonants: audiences have a right to hear what we have to say without needing to strain to do so.

VISUAL

Considerable research has been conducted on this aspect of communications and it will hardly surprise you to read that when we consider 'delivery', words are far less critical to your message than you might expect. Visual (what's seen) accounts for about half the impact on your audience and vocal accounts for only about a third! So, how you sound and how you look are very important components of your speech. Words are necessary but words alone don't make a presentation.

Eye contact is vitally important. When we talk to our family or our colleagues we look at them directly, yet when we speak to an audience we tend to avoid doing so. That's unnatural. Audiences expect to be talked *to* and not *at*!

This means that you must be sufficiently knowledgeable about your subject and familiar with your notes so that you are not dependent on the notes all the time. Your eye can take in several words or phrases at a time and you can then look up while addressing those. You can keep your finger moving down the side of your notes (which none of your audience will see) to make sure you don't get lost. But most people are far less dependent on their notes than they like to think. So look at your audience more than your notes. And if you do lose your place while looking at your audience, don't worry about it – just repeat the phrase with perhaps a bit more emphasis and it will appear intentional.

Remember, if you don't look directly at your listeners you cannot possibly 'read' how your speech is affecting them.

Do remember to be yourself when you get up to speak. One often sees speakers enjoy conversation and a cup of tea with people before they get up on the podium and once they stand up they put on a kind of severe mask. Don't do that. Be natural and friendly.

I always prefer to use a lectern, however simple, as this gives you somewhere safe to put your notes and it also looks more professional. But if you are standing on a podium, or behind a lectern, make sure you can be seen by all your audience.

You must appear confident and businesslike by standing (or sitting) up straight, not necessarily as though you are on a parade ground, but in such a way that you look alert and in command of the situation. A slouchy appearance with legs crossed and hands on hips, or worse still, hands folded, does not endear you to your audience.

HUMOUR

Over the years, course members have expressed anxiety over the use of humour. Humour in presentations is often grossly misunderstood. Humour *can* help if used sparingly and in the right places. But it should never be directed at one individual in, or any section of, your audience. Belittling members of your audience who may belong to a particular trade, profession or group is usually fatal. And the use of offensive humour is *always* taboo.

But we all feel more of a sense of unity when we laugh together and many barriers can be lowered by the judicious use of humour. But don't force it. If you are not naturally humorous then don't try to be. Whether or not you have a ready wit I advise against beginning your speech with a funny story. And never tell the audience you are about to relate something very amusing! They can, and will, decide whether or not they find it amusing.

I believe humour has best been described as being the icing on the cake rather than the cake itself.

CHECKLIST

1. *Be natural.* You should talk TO and not AT your audience.
2. *Look businesslike.* Stand, or sit, up straight.
3. *Don't keep looking at your notes all the time.* The audience expect to be looked at too.
4. *Vary the pitch, power and pace of your voice.* That's one of the most effective ways of keeping your listeners awake.
5. *Speak loud enough to be heard.* If more than a hundred people are present, use a microphone.
6. *Involve your audience as much as possible.* Listeners want to feel part of your presentation.
7. *Use humour sparingly.* And your humour should never offend.

CHAPTER SIX

Body language

Why don't th' feller who says, 'I'm no speechmaker',
let it go at that instead o' givin' a demonstration?

FRANK HUBBARD

Much has been written in recent years about body language and I suspect most of it is accurate. It has generally been accepted over the last twenty years that non-verbal aspects of communication play a far more important role than was previously recognised. Indeed, it is now generally accepted that 70% of communication exchanges are non-verbal or body language. The study of body language – also known as kinesics – is one of the newer behavioural science techniques.

YOUR BODY LANGUAGE

The person's body language about which you should be most concerned is your own! Your body and facial movements must be co-ordinated and they must be sensible and natural. Don't, therefore, shake your head while saying 'Yes' and don't grin when you say, 'I'm sorry'.

I don't believe personally that speakers need a great deal of tuition on their own body language, movement or gestures. When your mind and heart are in what you're saying your body will follow naturally. But you may have developed habits which are offputting

to others without even being aware of them. Scratchings, rubbings and pickings are all taboo. Men have a habit, immediately they get up to speak, of pulling up their trousers, checking their zip and straightening their tie. All of these minor adjustments should be taken care of before we stand up to speak. Men have a habit too of standing in the 'fig-leaf' position, hands held at crotch level, and sometimes they have the 'reverse fig-leaf' position where their hands are held behind their back for the entire speech. Both are unnatural and therefore wrong.

Empty your pockets before you speak, otherwise you may end up jingling your coins or keys, a sure sign to the audience that you're nervous. I've suggested earlier that you should always put your notes on a lectern – even a makeshift one – because holding notes in your hands when they are shaking like leaves is another indication of nervousness. All audiences expect you to be somewhat nervous but you don't need to show them just how nervous you really are! Women speakers should check a tendency to fiddle with a piece of jewellery or their hair.

THE AUDIENCE'S BODY LANGUAGE

As far as your audience is concerned it's probably best to accept that a reaction – any reaction – is better than indifference. At least your listeners are responding. An indifferent audience is the worst audience of all. These days you may find that many of your listeners have read books on body language or been on a body language course and so may tend to sit with their arms crossed, hands over mouth, their eyes closed or indeed they may demonstrate studied inattention which may include gazing at a high cloud passing the window or reading a document which has nothing to do with your presentation! They may 'threaten' you by frowning or engaging their neighbour in conversation. All you can do in such circum-stances is continue with good grace. Don't be deflected from your SPS by such behaviour even though it's difficult to cope with.

WATCH YOUR LISTENERS' REACTIONS

Do you notice the top brass crossing their legs and waggling the suspended toe when impatient? Then get your presentation moving faster into more interesting areas.

Those who sit with elbows on the table, hand over mouth, are suspending judgement.

If, during your speech, you see occasional frowns or puzzled looks, then you may need to give some further explanation of the point you're making. If it's a small audience, it may be worth your while asking the individual if he or she would like some further elucidation or information.

Beware of wearing distracting jewellery whether you're male or female. Huge chunky cufflinks, jangly bracelets, large belt buckles and huge earrings can distract and clatter. They can also make us look just a little shady!

Prospective customers generally prefer to buy from those with whom they can relate well. Therefore keep reminding them that you really are like them and use any information you have gleaned to show them you are on their side. Talk like them too.

Body language is not a replacement for words, but it does provide supplementary clues to understanding; and if you're going to speak on a regular basis it would be well worth your while attending a brief course on the subject or at least reading a book to get a general drift of the major points.

CHECKLIST

1. *Move naturally while you speak.* Don't cultivate some special 'speaking' stance or style. Be yourself.

2. *Don't show the audience that you are nervous.* Audiences expect

THE HENLEY COLLEGE LIBRARY

you to be somewhat nervous but don't keep rattling your keys or loose change as that will only call attention to how ill at ease you are.

3. *Make sure your body language matches what you're saying.* The words and music must harmonise.

4. *Eradicate off-putting habits.* Scratchings, rubbings, etc. are unacceptable.

5. *Watch your listeners' reactions.* Adjust your pace and explanations to what you see.

6. *Make sure there are no unsightly bulges or obvious outlines.* Nothing in your appearance or dress should distract your listeners from what you are saying.

CHAPTER SEVEN

Getting results

With words we govern men.

DISRAELI

For most people who read this book the object of their presentations will be to persuade. Apart perhaps from After Dinner speeches and talks which are given specifically to inform, each presentation should persuade your listeners to act in response to your SPS. If that's not the case there isn't much point in speaking in the first place.

TIMING

What you know about your subject, as we've said before, is highly important. But when considering your audience it's not just what *you* know that's important – it's what *they need to know*. You may be able to wax eloquently for hours on a particular topic but you won't have several hours before your audience in which to do so. *And one of the most vital elements in good speaking is timing.* Most presenters speak for far too long and some are irredeemably in love with the sound of their own voices.

We live in the age of the sound bite so no presentation from any one person should last more than forty minutes – fifty at the very most. If you find that what you need to say takes, say, seventy minutes, then give two presentations of thirty-five minutes each. It was Lord Brabazon of Tara who said, 'If what you have to say will

take more than twenty minutes then go away and write a book about it.'

You'll hardly ever get the desired result if you go overtime. The golden rule therefore is: *never, ever, go overtime*. Better still, if you have thirty minutes allotted for your speech take twenty-eight or twenty-nine. Audiences will warm to you for your consideration. If you plan properly you will never have to end with that tired cliché, 'Well, my time is up so I must bring this talk quickly to a close.'

RELEVANCE

You won't achieve the right result either if you keep talking about things only from your own perspective. As we said earlier *you must broaden your appeal to include your listeners and address their concerns, fears, hopes and interests.*

ACCURACY

You must always present *facts* not just *opinions*. When you state something as a fact it must be just that. We've all been to presentations where the speaker is dealing with a topic on which we are not generally expert but know a little about one or two of the areas being covered. If he or she makes a mistake in an area with which we are familiar our immediate reaction is to ask, 'If facts in this area are suspect, how do I know that the other facts are indeed correct?' The speaker's credibility is damaged, and most of us who speak don't, I'm afraid, have a great deal of spare credibility. So your facts must be correct – your opinions are only opinions. There is a time and place for opinions (which should always be *expressed* as opinions) but the balance of your speech must weigh heavily towards facts. Audiences can easily spot – and soon tire of – an opinionated speaker.

I know you'll say that what you have to get across is important – the changes which the company needs to make, the inspiration and motivation of your staff and so on. And you're absolutely right! But if you approach any audience from your point of view only, you will in all probability fail in your objective. Time and time again I've listened to people on courses and at conferences who approach everything either from their standpoint only or their company's standpoint. *Always* consider your audience: putting yourself in their shoes never fails to pay dividends.

And remember all audiences expect, and are entitled to expect:

- Explicit information
- Credible content
- Intelligent persuasion.

PHYSICAL ENVIRONMENT

To some it may seem a minor point, but the comfort of your audience is important. *Chairs* should be upright with support for arms if possible. They should be designed for all sizes of men and women in which to sit comfortably without difficulty. *Noise* should be at an absolute minimum. *Temperature* and *ventilation* are important too and the room should be *slightly* cooler than the temperature which people are used to in their own homes or offices. A hot room is always unpleasant and, after lunch, can often be disastrous! *Visibility* matters too: make sure the audience can see your flip chart, screen or displays. Don't block out what you want them to see by standing in front of it.

Having mentioned the above you will see that, once again, concern for your audience and their comfort is very important in your effort to persuade them to your way of thinking.

As far as *seating* your audience is concerned, it's better to have them close to you rather than scattered far away. This arrangement:

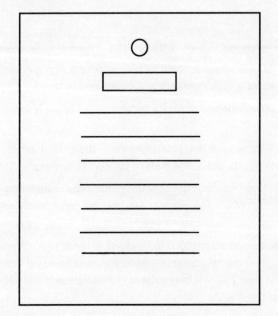

is preferable to this:

Keep your audience as close to you as is comfortable for both you and them. But do be careful you don't 'invade their space', especially in the early part of your speech, by coming around from the lectern and talking too closely to them or touching them. Audiences need to know a speaker well and have warmed to him or her before either of these practices is acceptable.

I always recommend that, wherever possible, you leave a 'Reserved' sign on the back two rows of chairs so that those who come after you have begun speaking can take their places in those two rows. This greatly minimises disruption throughout your talk and also causes latecomers the least amount of embarrassment as their late entry is hardly noticed by the remainder of your audience.

Finally, you should look the part by dressing smartly – not by being overdressed. I generally recommend that a speaker dresses just slightly more formally than the audience, although I certainly accept that in workshop sessions or in addressing factory workers, for example, an informal approach is likely to be far more acceptable.

─────────────── **CHECKLIST** ───────────────

1. *Never go overtime.* Audiences hate speakers who go overtime and in any event it is monumentally discourteous to do so.

2. *Check your information for its accuracy.* To know is better than to guess.

3. *Present facts and not just opinions.* There is a place for your opinions but it's not in the body of your presentation.

4. *Always think of your presentation from the standpoint of your audience.* When you do this you are far more likely to present information relevant to their needs.

5. *Keep noise and distractions to an absolute minimum.* The audience are hardly likely to appreciate what you have to say if they have to strain to hear you or if they suffer continual distractions either visual or aural.

6. *Arrange the room so that your audience are reasonably close to you and to each other.* An audience that is spread far and wide is far more difficult to manage.

7. *Ensure your audience are comfortable.* This applies to furnishings, spacing and room temperature.

8. *Dress the part.* Share their culture wherever possible.

CHAPTER EIGHT

Visual aids

All my shows are great. Some of them are bad,
but they're all great.

———

LORD GRADE

To list all the various modern visual aids available and describe their details and variations in this short book would be impossible. But the following points will help you to avoid the major pitfalls in using any visual aids. Visual aids can usually enhance any presentation *but*, if not handled properly, they can often detract from what is said; and, if handled badly, can turn your speech into a nightmare!

USING VISUAL AIDS EFFECTIVELY

———

There are three requirements for effective visual aids:

- They must fit the setting in which the presentation is being given
- They must support your message
- They must be used in moderation.

One *picture* is indeed worth a thousand words but speakers forget that we ourselves are our best visual aid which is why preachers stand in pulpits and politicians stand on soapboxes. But what audiences often see instead of a picture is a few dozen slides in a thirty-minute presentation most of which are rows and rows of

words which are read by the speaker *and* the audience. Or, worse still, rows and rows of figures with zillions of zeros because there is no legend at the top of the slide.

What we also forget is that most audiences can read from our slides about three times as fast as we can speak – *and they do!* Remember the eye always takes precedence over the ear. Therefore, don't compete with your acetate or slide. Make your point and then say, 'Let me illustrate what I mean', or 'As you can see here . . .'. While the audience are looking at your slide *don't SAY anything.* It has been claimed that a great deal of expensive senior management time is spent in meetings – I believe equally large blocks of time are spent by the same people narrating slide shows. To compound the problem, a speaker often reads from slides which are reproduced in handouts. The whole effect is deadly. *Visual aids should always speak for themselves.*

But there are occasions when words can and should be used and indeed in considering a piece of legislation or an extract from a legal document it is right and proper that they are. But words don't inspire; they don't motivate; they are, well, just words! And if you must have slides with words – in outlining a public relations campaign, for example – then have a maximum of eight lines per slide and no more than twenty-five characters per line.

Except in the most unusual circumstances (working through a plan of a building complex perhaps, or a set of Annual Accounts), leave all your handouts on your lectern or table until your presentation is finished. *Then* hand them out to your audience.

TYPES OF VISUAL AID

In general terms you will have a choice of four types of visual aid:

- *The flip chart* – useful when we wish the audience to participate. We ask a question, for example, and record the answers.
- *The overhead projector* (OHP) – useful for explanations; very often used to good effect in lectures.

- *Slides* – normally used in formal presentations. Probably the visual aid which is misused more than any other!
- *Videos* – used in 'persuasive' situations. Very effective but expensive to produce.

Visual aids – videos, overhead projectors (OHPs), slides, flip charts, computer graphics – all should be used to clarify, expand or *show* something which is not easily described. They can be invaluable when statistical or numerical data are involved or where medical or scientific procedures are being presented. Organisational relationships can also be displayed to good effect as can *simple* graphs, bar charts and histograms.

OVERALL GUIDELINES

The overall guiding rule is this: always plan your speech first and *then* ask yourself if a visual aid or two would help support your message or awaken your audience. In other words, use visual aids only if you have to and don't ever use any visual aid just because it's available, especially if it's available from some previous presentation given either by you or someone else in the company.

Whether your organisation is large or small, your visual aids should be professionally produced. It costs money but it prevents your giving a kind of 'Mickey Mouse' image of your organisation.

As speakers we're all different. We look different, we sound different, our method of speaking is different. Happily, this means that we'll be listened to for at least five minutes however badly we present – just because we're different. Don't therefore rush to put your visual aids up the moment you begin to speak. Establish your own authority and effectiveness and *then* put up your first visual whether you are using the simple flip chart, the OHP or slides.

Just a few points in conclusion to help you avoid the most common mistakes in using visual aids:

- Make sure you write large enough letters so your writing can be clearly seen and comprehended by all your listeners.

- Make sure ALL your visual aids are large enough to be seen by everybody in the room; and don't block out any section of the screen.

- Don't talk as you write. Confiding in the flip chart is not speaking to your audience.

- There's a great and natural temptation for us to look at the screen. Don't. Everything you write or display on the OHP is guaranteed to come up behind you on the screen. If using slides, it is acceptable to glance occasionally at the screen to check that the correct slide is showing, but don't keep admiring your celluloid as though it were a Constable. (There is a device available now which displays simultaneously on your lectern the slide which is appearing on the screen, thus obviating the need ever to glance behind you, even for a moment.)

- Always explain whatever you show on screen and, once explained, remove it.

- If you use a pointer, point precisely at whatever it is you are discussing, then fold the pointer up and put it down. And don't whatever you do, try using one of those torches with a little white arrow: you'll never manage to point it at anything without the arrow shaking or drifting all over the place. Use a modern laser pointer instead.

An engineer once told me that 'no piece of machinery with moving parts never breaks down'. And how right he was. Remember, therefore, that something may indeed go wrong and go wrong through no fault of yours. You must always go to any presentation prepared for the worst, that is to say, you may have to go ahead without your precious visual aids. There's no way any book, or I suspect any individual, can tell you how to do that but you must keep the thought in the back of your mind. You can't invite 200 people to a talk and then cancel it just because your projector isn't working! So you simply explain the circumstances and press on. It won't be as good but at least you won't waste the time of those who may have come a long distance to hear you. So be prepared, thereby avoiding total catastrophe.

As already mentioned there's an enormous range of visual aids available to speakers and you should make yourself aware of what you can hire or buy. But do be careful about being too 'glitzy'. Your listeners are there to hear you and remember what you've said, not to go away commenting on how marvellous and slick your machinery appeared to be.

REHEARSAL

Whenever your presentation includes visual aids you must always rehearse. This is particularly so if the room is large and you'll be assisted by a projectionist or whenever a team presentation is involved. I've never discovered why, but it's fiendishly difficult to get people to approach a rehearsal with anything other than the most grudging co-operation. But the rehearsal, apart from helping everyone see exactly where they fit into the whole scheme of things, is the last chance you'll all have to spot and correct those small, but often embarrassing, mistakes which creep into most presentations.

It goes without saying that if you're speaking outside your own premises you should arrive early, check the position and workings of the equipment and the screen positions. Make sure the focus is right, make sure your visual aids can be seen from the back of the room, check how to control the room lighting and so on. Time spent in last-minute preparation ahead of your presentation is *never* wasted.

Finally, it's estimated that if we *say, and then show*, retention is increased by about 80%; so visual aids which fit the setting, which are used at the right time and in moderation can greatly enhance your presentation and give it a much more professional touch. So, find out what's on the market now (equipment, computer graphics, etc.) that will help make your presentation as memorable and professional as you wish it to be.

CHECKLIST
---

1. *Use visual aids only if they support your SPS.*   Never show anything which is not *strictly* relevant to the purpose you're trying to achieve.

2. *Use your visual aids in moderation.*   Too many acetates, slides and videos end up becoming a distraction from your main message.

3. *Don't use any visual aid just because you have it to hand.*   Always ask, 'Is this really necessary?' Better still, 'Does it show what I cannot say?'

4. *Use 'visual verbals' sparingly.*   There is a place for them sometimes but not in every single speech you give.

5. *Never turn your back on your listeners.*   It's rude and in any event you lose control of any audience when you fail to face them directly.

6. *Find out from the specialist suppliers what's available that can enhance your speech AND is easy and efficient to use.*   New and helpful products come on the market frequently, particularly in the area of computer graphics.

7. *A rehearsal is vital when using visual aids.*   Their use, while often adding much to your presentation, also adds greatly to the possibility of its becoming a shambles!

CHAPTER NINE

Dealing with nervousness

I believe that anyone can conquer fear by doing the things he fears to do, provided he keeps doing them until he gets a record of successful experiences behind him.

———

ELEANOR ROOSEVELT

We all have various levels of confidence in our lives. For some, talking to people, especially people they hardly know, is a daunting task. For many, the very thought of giving a speech of any kind makes them apprehensive and diffident. Their language becomes impersonal and even cold and their demeanour stiff and un-approachable. The last thing they want to be is 'themselves'.

When we are very nervous we become obsessed with concern over what the audience is thinking about us, little realising that they never think about us as much as we imagine. Nervousness, like income tax, will never go away. Nor should it. If you don't feel a sense of occasion every time you speak in public you'll cease to be any good at it. All great speakers are nervous. But there's a difference between being nervous and being petrified. And there's a difference between being nervous and feeling a sense of occasion.

The more we speak the less nervous we become – practice really does make perfect. But we must never lose the feeling that speaking in public does have its demands and its risks. And incidentally, although a huge audience initially looks frightening the 'butterflies' for the most part disappear after a minute or so. It's the small

audience you need to be more concerned about; and, indeed, the worst audience of all comprises about six to eight of your peers.

So don't think just because you are nervous something is wrong with you – quite the opposite is true. We all have butterflies. The trick is to get them flying in formation. And if you don't have some slight apprehension and a sense of occasion when you have to give a speech then you will in all probability do a poor job.

Here then are eight simple keys to help you overcome unnecessary nerves.

1. Make sure you are properly prepared with at least one rehearsal. That means you stand up and rehearse your speech in your home or office. You deliver it exactly as you will on the day or night and don't just mumble it like some Eastern mystic! On the day it will usually be about 10% longer than at the rehearsal. If a team is presenting you should, if at all possible, rehearse twice. Unless it's a shambles you should not rehearse more than twice, otherwise it will tend to become boring to you and you will have difficulty in sounding fresh when you do stand up to speak. If you are ill-prepared you will always feel extremely nervous, and deservedly so.

2. Have proper notes which can be easily read wherever you need to place them – on a table, on your briefcase, on a lectern or if you have to hold them throughout your speech.

3. Take six or ten deep breaths *before* you get up to speak – not *as* you get up to speak, otherwise you will present both an unusual appearance and an offputting sound. No one quite knows what this does other than oxygenate the lungs but it does help calm our nerves while under stress.

4. Never regard the audience as your enemy. They're not. At worst they are probably neutral but if you treat them as your enemy, you will be guilty of a self-fulfilling prophecy. All audiences want to spend their time profitably so they really do want you to give them an interesting speech. And they don't quite know what to do or say when a speaker bungles his or her assignment. So they really are basically on your side.

5. Look at the friendlier members of your audience. Almost all audiences contain people who look like Ghengis Khan! Spend less time looking at those. But don't stare at any particular individuals. Looking at the friendlier ones will give you confidence and encouragement. And don't assume (as many inexperienced speakers do) that because someone appears to be somewhat less than wildly enthusiastic about absolutely everything you are saying that he or she violently disagrees with you. S/he may have a health problem; s/he may be worried or concerned over some business or private matter; or s/he may – surprise, surprise – be just thinking about what you are saying and weighing it up in his/her mind. Or perhaps s/he's formulating a question to ask at the end of your speech.

6. Each of us is unique, and because of that, we'll be listened to for several minutes just because we are different from every other speaker your listeners have heard from before.

7. Do not think of your self-image. Don't try to become a different personality or put on an act. Be yourself. Think only of the message (the SPS) you are trying to put across. Remember if you weren't there to give it somebody else would do so!

8. Pause occasionally to collect your thoughts and especially at the transitions from one point to another. Give yourself and the audience a bit of breathing space – novices rush through their talks at breathtaking speed. Take your time. If you have rehearsed you'll know how long it takes: use that time and no more.

Finally, don't ever drink alcohol to overcome nervousness – that's fatal. A drink perhaps on a very hot day may be acceptable but never consume large quantities of alcohol before giving a serious speech or presentation.

CHECKLIST
---

1. *The feeling or nervousness will never leave you.* Nor should it! If you don't experience at least a sense of occasion when you have to speak you'll never be a successful speaker.

2. *So, some nervousness is good for you.* It will keep you on your toes.

3. *Breathe deeply before you begin to speak.* It really does help calm your nerves.

4. *Never let the audience see how nervous you are.* And on no account should you tell them you're dreading the whole performance!

5. *Small groups are more difficult to address than large audiences.* So don't ever make the mistake of thinking that just because it's a small group you don't need to prepare thoroughly.

6. *Use ALL of the eight keys listed to help you control nervousness.* They sound simple and they are, but they do work.

7. *Never drink alcohol before you make a business presentation.* That advice applies, in my view, to *ALL* presentations but is particularly important when you are pitching for new business or representing your company or organisation.

8. *Practice really does make perfect.* And it's the same with any skill one seeks to acquire.

CHAPTER TEN

Dealing with questions and objections

A good listener is not only popular everywhere,
but after a while he gets to know something.

WILSON MIZNER

The way you deal with questions after your presentation really is highly important. I've seen many very good presentations ruined by the shoddy performance of speakers once they have to face their audience over questions. And, to be fair, I've watched some poor pitches redeemed by the competent manner in which questions were dealt with.

PREPARATION

As part of the general preparation for your speech, once you've finished drafting it, you should think of the type of questions you may be asked. This is all part of the process of putting yourself in the place of your listeners. If you take some time to discuss the topic with a colleague or two they'll often come up with questions which may well arise. And, if you have addressed the subject previously, you will (or should!) have noted the questions you were asked then so that you will have your answers ready.

TECHNIQUE

On most of my courses, delegates have handled questions poorly
– even though they knew the answers! There are several reasons
for this. The suggestions which follow, if adopted, will help you
enormously in handling this aspect of your talks.

It's a good idea to tell your audience when you will accept
questions and how you propose to deal with them. In small
audiences people can simply interrupt or raise their hands but in
larger audiences you need to establish precisely how people are to
put questions or objections. In general terms, questions should be
taken after each separate section in which they are generated
otherwise the context is lost and some may forget the point you
were making earlier on in the presentation.

The main problem arises from the fact that many of us have not
developed as we should the habit of listening to others. We *think*
we listen but in reality we don't. Too often we listen for *what WE
want to hear*. In business communications that's fatal. Listening
attentively sends a signal to your audience that you're interested in
them and in what they have to say. So always *listen* carefully to
what your questioner (or contributor) is actually saying. He or she
may ask a very poor question, the question may be muddled, the
questioner may ask it in very much the wrong attitude, it may be
a loaded question, the questioner may just be trying to catch you
out, he or she may even agree with all that you said, but the one
thing above all else that your questioner needs is to be listened to.
He or she needs to know that they have been heard and that you
comprehend what was said. So you must show that you have heard
and understood. You can do this by nodding your head slightly as
the question is being asked or by smiling or perhaps having an
expression of genuine concern.

Don't *EVER* put your questioner down or give any indication
through your body language, or what you say, that you regard the
question as stupid. We've all been in situations where we have

wanted to ask a question but felt embarrassed because it seemed too elementary and by asking it we would demonstrate our ignorance for all the world to see. But how often have we found someone else in the audience asked 'our' question? And we've all blurted out questions and then one nanosecond later have realised that we – and probably everyone else present – know the answer!! In all such circumstances we appreciate a courteous reply. *Your* questioners will too.

So first you *listen*. You then *define* the question.

In larger groups it's usual to thank the questioner (without using that patronising form of words 'That's a very good question') and repeat the question so that others can hear it. You can preface your response by saying, 'Let me be sure I understand the point you're making' or 'Am I correct in understanding that you are particularly concerned about . . . ?' This simple procedure shows you have comprehended the question and it also gives you a few extra seconds to think on your feet. (Some speakers seem to think *with* their feet but that's not quite so effective!) Even though you may understand the question clearly this shows the audience you are a good listener too. It also prevents your making a hasty statement which may not address the question properly.

Having listened and defined, you then *recognise*. By recognise is meant telling the questioner that he or she has made an interesting point, or has given some thought to the proposition, or is obviously drawing on experience in raising that particular issue. If you like, it 'gives value to the question and the questioner' by showing you you need to think before answering it.

Some people have difficulty in making themselves clear when they speak especially when they're asking questions. So just listen to what they are trying to say and answer the underlying query rather than their actual words. Always try and find something to commend whenever you are asked an unusual or rather extraordinary question.

So, having listened, defined and recognised, finally, you *answer*.

But what happens if you don't know the answer? Never pretend that you do. As we grow older (and wiser) we realise that we don't, nor can we be expected to, know absolutely everything about our subject. Most of our listeners realise that no one has all the answers on any subject at split-second command. So the reply you give on every occasion where you don't know the answer is this: 'I'm sorry, I just don't know the answer to that one.'

You should, however, make some effort to direct your questioner to where the information may be found or, better still, volunteer to find out the information and send it on to him or her. (But if you make such a promise do fulfil it.) You can also ask another member of your team, or indeed the audience themselves, if they know the answer. But never try to 'wing it'. There'll always be someone in the room who really *does* know the answer and will happily expose your non-answer for the sham it is!

Don't try to evade any issue and if something is raised which you are not at liberty to answer just say so. 'We don't have all the information on that occurrence yet' or 'You will understand that at this delicate stage in negotiations I am unable to comment on that right now' are often acceptable provided of course they represent the truth. When being questioned, always smile and look interested. Don't fidget. Look directly at the questioner, but when answering look at him/her occasionally but also at your entire audience too.

In answering questions there are two golden rules which you must never forget:

1. Never answer any question quickly, especially the simple question.
2. What you say in response must be the truth. (It does not necessarily have to be *all* the truth. but whatever you actually say must be the truth.)

If there is a genuine objection to what you've said then you must admit its validity. But you should minimise its importance and again state that the benefits of what you propose far outweigh the disadvantages. If someone objects to something you have said and s/he's right you can graciously say, 'Thank you for bringing that to my attention. I was not aware of that most recent piece of research.' But dealing with genuinely felt objections demands diplomacy, discernment and, dare I say, a degree of humility. Don't get into a fight – you may win that particular battle but you'll lose the war.

If you're pitching for business and someone points out a weakness in your organisation, just admit it and say something like, 'Yes, we're aware of that, and are taking steps to put it right.' And don't 'knock' another company, firm or product. You lose nothing with an intelligent audience when you admit other organisations have strong points too. And you should obviously go on to show the advantages of your own product or service.

Loaded questions will often have a presumption which is an error right at the beginning. Make sure you correct this error before answering the question. Indeed sometimes when the error is corrected there's really no question left. Occasionally, questions may be so outrageous that they really don't demand an answer at all.

For any successful presentation you must have the audience on your side; so if you are subject to hostile questioning never snap back at your questioner. Always treat him or her with courtesy and eventually the audience will come on to your side. If you make your questioners feel small or stupid, not only will they resent your conduct but others listening will do so too.

And finally, remember that the answer to every single question should further the aim of your SPS. Indeed questions often allow you to give further information which you didn't have time to present in your speech – and if the audience keep asking questions, they can't blame you for going overtime!

━━━━━━━━━━━━━━━━━━━━ **CHECKLIST** ━━━━━━━━━━━━

1. *Think of as many questions as you can in advance and have your answers already prepared.* While you probably won't be able to come up with every possible question you will be able to answer most people confidently.

2. *Questions are an important part of most presentations* Business can often be gained or lost by the manner in which questions and objections are handled.

3. *Never put a questioner down in any business presentation.* You gain absolutely nothing by making someone else feel embarrassed. And if you do make them feel embarrassed they'll remember you — for all the wrong reasons.

4. *Listen carefully to every question.* Don't listen for what you think the questioner is asking or indeed should be asking: listen to what he or she actually asks.

5. *Having listened, then define, recognise and answer.* Never rush the answer to any question.

6. *'I don't know' is, on occasion, a perfectly good answer.* But offer to send on the requested information as soon as possible.

7. *ALL answers must further the specific aim of your presentation.* Don't get sidetracked.

━━━━━━━━━━━━━━━━━━━━━━━━━━━━━━━━━━━━━

THE HENLEY COLLEGE LIBRARY

CHAPTER ELEVEN

The media interview

'If everybody minded their own business', the Duchess said in a hoarse growl, 'the world would go round a deal faster than it does.'

——

'ALICE IN WONDERLAND'

We're all well aware of the media revolution: there are more newspapers, magazines, radio and television outlets than ever before. And the revolution is going to continue. It follows therefore that many company directors and senior executives will have to appear on television and give the occasional radio or press interview.

It is simply impossible to impart the skills necessary for any of these activities through the pages of a short (or even a long) book. If you know you are going to have to give interviews on a regular basis you should attend a specialist course to get the feel of the kind of pressure you will be under and to build your confidence through expert tuition. But the following few rules *will* help you in all such situations although do remember they are not exhaustive. They'll assist in the occasional interview but you should not agree to give regular interviews without first having expert tuition.

BASIC TECHNIQUES
——

Most interviews, particularly TV and radio, are all about credibility and impressions. If you don't come across as a credible spokesperson

for your company, it hardly matters what you have to say because
your listeners won't believe you nor will they want to listen to you.
Viewers remember general impressions far more than specific facts.
What you look and sound like are therefore highly important and
will remain in the minds of your viewers and listeners far longer
than what you actually say.

- Therefore, always look at your interviewer.
- Use conversational tones.
- Don't slouch – lean slightly forward.
- And don't wriggle around in your chair nor should you fidget.
- Don't touch the microphone.
- If possible, sip water throughout the interview – your mouth will
  invariably become dry when you're under pressure.
- Don't just react to questions you are asked. Interviewers like
  people who are full of life, ideas and information.
- Often the time for interviews is limited; indeed, the average
  interview takes up less than three minutes! You must therefore
  have firmly in mind two or three points you are going to make,
  come what may. If you are not so prepared the confusion and
  pressure may make your mind go blank or you will give long
  rambling answers, lapse into jargon or make mildly incoherent
  statements. So have two or three 'punchy' items you are going
  to put across whatever happens.
- Don't use negative words when answering – always be positive.
  If *you* use only positive words then these are the only words
  which can be attributed to you.
- If your interviewer starts a question with an incorrect assertion
  or information, make sure these are corrected – courteously but
  firmly – before you proceed to answer the question. Often, once
  the incorrect 'facts' have been put right, there's no real question
  left.
- Remember: nothing you say is 'off the record'.
- Remember too that if there are any skeletons in your organisation's cupboard, they'll probably be dragged out in full view. Be

prepared. I always recommend that you have a crisis plan ready on which all responsible managers and employees are well briefed. Indeed *all* important company policies should be formulated on an ongoing basis so that everyone involved knows what may be revealed in a media interview. I recommend too that you have one or two colleagues 'pre-grill' you, just as the interviewer will, so that you have reasonable and agreed answers ready. It's a very good idea to think of the five or six questions you would least like to be asked and have your answers ready for those.

- Never lie and never say, 'No comment.' There are probably good reasons why you feel you cannot comment at the time, so just say what they are.

- Don't engage in verbal sparring with any interviewer: you'll probably lose.

- And it goes without saying that you should never lose your temper with an interviewer or get drawn into long rambling side issues.

- Don't be put off by silences either. Silence is a very powerful weapon in many business/interviewing situations. The golden rule is: *never speak unless it's an improvement on silence.*

- Overall, have a positive attitude.

- And always have a de-briefing afterwards. We can all gain much from honest constructive criticism. It can hurt, I know, but it pays huge dividends in the communication process.

CHECKLIST

1. *Undergo training if you expect to be interviewed regularly.* Answering questions in media interviews is not for the fainthearted.

2. *Be positive.* If you use only positive words then only positive words are recorded.

3. *Don't allow yourself to be flustered.* Keep to the point and be brief.

4. *Make your points, come what may.* Always have two or three positive points which you are determined to put across.

5. *Have a few people in your office 'pre-grill' you before the interview.* Getting into an atmosphere where you face tough questioning can be very helpful.

6. *Always hold a de-briefing session afterwards.* Learn from your experience, whether it's been good or bad.

CHAPTER TWELVE

After Dinner speaking

The human brain starts working the moment you are born
and never stops until you stand up to speak in public.

SIR GEORGE JESSEL

I believe that probably the most difficult speech for any businessman
or businesswomen is the After Dinner speech. One reason for this
is that we are often expected to entertain – and we are not
entertainers: our lives are spent instead in directing and managing
companies and other organisations.

The After Dinner speech requires the same careful construction
as any other speech we make and it certainly needs at least one
rehearsal.

TIMING

For some unknown reason After Dinner speaking seems to lend
itself to the most appalling timing on a consistent basis. If you are
not a particularly good speaker your speech should last about five
minutes. If you are fairly good at this kind of speech then eight
minutes should be about right. And if you are extremely competent
ten minutes is acceptable – just.

But under no circumstances, on any formal occasion, should you
ever take longer than ten minutes for an After Dinner speech. Late

in the evening, after a heavy meal, when you are one of two, three or maybe even four speakers people's attention span is particularly short. I've seen many people attempt an After Dinner speech of up to twenty minutes' duration and they have in every single instance lost their audience entirely. Besides any considerations of boredom/ennui, people have trains to catch and perhaps long journeys to make with an early start the following morning and it is being highly inconsiderate to keep them listening for longer than is appropriate.

You'll often be told by the person responsible for the evening that you are not to exceed a certain time limit. And if you're not told, ask.

THE BASIC RULES

Graciousness and courtesy are highly important in this environment but this does not mean one should be insincere. Normally, one refers to the occasion, the principal people present and if you are, for example, proposing the toast to The Guests you will refer directly to a number of them and their achievements or association with your organisation or the function itself. But don't try to mention every guest by name if there are dozens present. Such long lists bore very easily. If you are replying for The Guests you would obviously refer to the food, wine and perhaps the setting besides the host organisation and its Master, President or Chairman.

You should not try to be hilariously funny. On such occasions the best jokes are usually impromptu. Some people tend to string a number of not very funny stories together – of the 'have you heard the one about' variety. Any story, quotation, or anecdote should have *relevance* to the occasion. Stories should not be told out of context just because *you* think they have humorous appeal.

Remember, too, to think clearly about the atmosphere and the occasion. City dinners are fairly formal affairs, as are annual dinners of Professional and Trade associations. Regimental dinners are formal too but there's often more of a sense of fun at those. Old

Girls or Old Boys Reunion dinners are more relaxed affairs. But whether formal or informal don't use long words if you know shorter ones that mean the same thing and don't try to impress your audience by the use of ornate and pompous words or phrases. I've heard many a speaker put on some kind of pompous voice when speaking at dinners where important people are present. Don't. Be yourself. Make sure your grammar, diction and so on are in order as you would giving any other speech but don't involve yourself in some pretence.

If it is a very formal occasion you will need to get the preamble or allocution right. The Toastmaster will usually help you in this but if there is no Toastmaster present then it is your responsibility to get it right so that you mention everyone in the correct order.

In times gone by there were often six speeches following a formal dinner. These days there are normally just two, three or four. The toasts are usually either to The Guests or The Company and one replies to these toasts depending on whether one is host or guest.

Remember, the lower down you come in the toast list, the greater the premium on brevity. With our listeners goodwill evaporates, literally, by the minute!

━━━━━━━━━━━━━━━━━ **CHECKLIST** ━━━━━━━━━━━━━━━

1. *Be brief.* Late in the evening, goodwill evaporates by the minute.

2. *Be relevant.* Every story or anecdote should have some connection with the function or organisation.

3. *Don't try to be a comedian.* Use amusing or witty stories if (a) they're relevant and (b) you have no real difficulty in telling a funny story.

4. *Graciousness and courtesy are important.* They cost nothing and always create the right impression.

5. *Get the protocol right first time.* If you don't know it, ask someone who does.

6. *For the second time — be brief!* Your audience will love you if you are!

CHAPTER THIRTEEN

Special occasions

Tact is the knack of making a point without
making an enemy.

HOWARD W. NEWTON

RETIREMENT PRESENTATIONS

At one time or another in our business lives most of us will have
to make a retirement presentation to a colleague or employee. Like
all speeches this one too must be prepared.

It should last no longer than ten minutes and should never
exaggerate the attainments of the individual retiring nor, on the
other hand, should it overlook the contribution he/she has made to
the company. It's important to remember that it may be an
emotional occasion for the person retiring although it is less usual
these days for someone to spend their entire working life with a
single employer.

Tell some amusing stories by all means; and it is permissible on
these occasions to poke some gentle fun at the person retiring but
not, however, in any way which would demean him or her in the
eyes of colleagues. Thank him/her for his/her contribution to the
company during his/her employment. And don't forget his or her
partner too who in many cases will have been a support during his/
her career – sometimes at considerable personal inconvenience.

If you're making a physical presentation of a gift then, if possible, go over and join the recipient immediately afterwards to avoid those awkward moments when people just stand in the middle of a room not knowing quite what to do next.

Finally, tell your retiring colleague s/he's welcome back as a visitor from time to time but do specify which occasions are appropriate. The last thing we want in a busy life are visitors turning up unexpectedly at the worst possible time during a hectic day!

Again, the retirement speech should last no more than ten minutes.

INTRODUCING OTHER SPEAKERS

When you are introducing another speaker, remember it is the other speaker whom the audience have come to hear, not you! This is not therefore the occasion for you to expand your own ego. Your specific purpose is twofold: to make the audience want to hear the speaker and to make the speaker feel welcome.

Your introduction should be short – usually two minutes is just about right. Tell the audience something about the speaker that they may not already know. Don't go overboard in listing achievements but do mention the points which are particularly relevant to the particular audience. It's often a good idea to let the speaker know the points you intend alluding to. Sometimes for the very best of reasons people prefer some aspects of their lives or achievements to remain private.

Find out how to pronounce your visitor's name and write it down. I've known of speakers to be introduced by the wrong name entirely and in one unfortunate incident by the name of someone already deceased!

VOTES OF THANKS

This is one of the very few speeches which you don't need to prepare entirely in advance. Again, it should be brief: about a minute and a half is ideal.

Mention some items from the speech which you found particularly interesting or perhaps were unaware of previously. This shows, among other things, that you listened to what was said.

Never disagree with the speaker or put him or her down. If they are your guests they are entitled to be treated with courtesy and in any event most speakers won't expect everybody to agree with all they have to say – and some are delightfully controversial as a matter of course.

If appropriate, express the hope that the speaker might perhaps be your guest on some future occasion. And you should always start the applause, asking the audience to join with you in so doing.

LOYAL TOASTS

The Loyal Toast is almost always proposed by the chairman of the lunch or dinner and consists of just two words, 'The Queen'. Many try to be flowery here and add bits and pieces. Don't. 'The Queen': these two words alone are correct.

Sometimes there's an additional toast, 'The Royal Family'. The exact wording is issued officially from Buckingham Palace and will usually be printed on your menu. Again, only the precise words printed should be spoken.

If you are proposing a toast to any of Her Majesty's Forces there will need to be a patriotic ring about what you say, but don't overdo this. You should be quietly sincere. If you have served in the forces yourself then a bit of humour is appropriate, and just a bit of inter-service chaffing is acceptable. If you haven't served then the humour should be sparing. There is plenty of history on which to draw and numerous quotations that are highly effective. Remember to pay tribute to the auxiliary services too whenever it's appropriate to do so.

SEMINARS, CONFERENCES, ETC.

Just a word to remind you that timing is all if you are one of a number of speakers. It takes just one or two speakers to go overtime and the whole performance becomes a shambles.

Do remember it is essential that you find out what *precise* aspects of the subject your colleagues on the platform will be covering and that you tell them the points you will be addressing. It's notoriously difficult to get this information, I realise (mainly because people flatly refuse to prepare in advance!) but if the seminar is to be a success all speakers must give value for money and not repeat what others have said.

Remember too that while you are part of a group of speakers on a platform you are just as much part of the team when you are not speaking as when you are. Therefore don't look bored, shake your head, giggle or do anything else to distract attention from the speaker. Give him or her your undivided attention throughout, difficult though that might be, especially if you have heard it all several times before!

BAD NEWS AND GOOD NEWS

There will inevitably be occasions when bad news has to be presented, often to colleagues and staff. In a difficult situation, any company which has satisfactory relations with its employees will find them useful allies. An external threat can unify almost any group.

If you are presenting bad news you must show that you too are affected by it and that you care. Any flippancy or offhand comment on such occasions is deadly and deserve the scorn they will reap. Be sensitive. There are times when a silver lining can be seen or when good can come from difficult circumstances but be careful – don't claim to see silver linings when there aren't any. If possible always offer support to those affected by bad news and whatever you do remember that what you say must be the truth. And make sure you speak to those affected before a rumour takes hold. Don't fudge and don't trivialise. If it's possible to end on an upbeat note without adversely affecting what you have to say, do so.

Good news is easier to deliver. Make sure you *sound* as though you are giving good news. And always remember to share the credit and thank those principally responsible.

SPEAKING OVERSEAS

Nancy Mitford is alleged to have said, 'Abroad is unutterably bloody and foreigners are fiends'. If that's *your* view you won't be a great hit if you speak overseas! But many of us have to.

It goes without saying that courtesy to your hosts and their country is essential and should be expressed. It's also appropriate to ask an expert on the country what pitfalls to avoid. Even the UK and the US are divided by the same language. Be prepared to adjust. Cultural barriers are important and we can offend without having the slightest intention of doing so. There are countries which are classified as 'high context', such as France, Spain, Greece, China, etc., and others which are 'low context' such as Sweden, Switzerland, Germany, the UK and the US. Those in 'high context' countries communicate far more by nuance than we do and are therefore less dependent on the spoken word. In the Orient, looking at people directly in the eye can be off-putting for them, and others smile, nod and make polite noises not because they are in agreement but to encourage you to continue. Observe how the audience responds to other speakers and then you are less likely to be caught off guard.

It's always most useful to speak a few words of their language at the beginning and end of your speech – much better of course if you speak their language fluently! And if you can honestly compliment your overseas listeners on some aspect of their culture, country or business then do so. But don't sound patronising or condescending.

CHECKLIST

---

1. *Do lots of research for speeches on special occasions.* They're all slightly different.

2. *Be as sincere as you can.* You owe this to your audience especially if you are their guest.

3. *Be yourself, whether at home or abroad.* Don't put on any special 'dignified' voice.

4. *Use humour sparingly and never disparagingly.* Humour is the icing on the cake, not the cake itself.

5. *Be particularly careful of the content AND timing when taking part in a conference or seminar.* You owe this to your fellow speakers as well as your audience.

CHAPTER FOURTEEN

The main pitfalls

It is a luxury to be understood.

———

EMERSON

Here are ten cardinal pitfalls to be avoided at all costs. My intention is for these to become your checklist for every speech you make in future. Even if everything else is forgotten the avoidance of these errors will put you head and shoulders above the average speaker. They're all expressed in the negative because *all* are to be avoided.

1. Poorly defined Specific Purpose Statement.
2. Lack of thorough preparation.
3. Poor analysis of your audience.
4. Speaking in a listless deadpan manner.
5. Humour, whether thought appropriate or not, being forced into a speech for effect.
6. Using 'wordy' visual aids.
7. Having far too many (and complicated) visual aids.
8. Going on and on about concluding and never quite doing so.
9. Going overtime.
10. Failing to evaluate your performance after the speech.

Index

accuracy of facts 43–4, 46
action step 25
Adams, Franklin P. 19
After Dinner speaking 77–80
   basic rules 79–80
   timing 77, 79
alcohol 60, 61
analysis of audience 16, 17, 89
anecdotes 21, 79, 80
annual dinners 79
answering questions *see* questions
appearance 38, 39
articulation 32
attention of audience 16
   attention step 25
audience
   analysis of 16, 17, 89
   and bad news 85–6
   behaviour of 29
   body language of 37–8, 39
   caring for 11
   changing attitudes of 8
   culture of 17, 47, 86
   empathy with 44, 46
   expectations of 7, 31, 44
   holding attention 16, 25
   hostile 37
   interests and concerns of 17, 43
   involving 16, 17, 31, 34
   knowledge of 11–18
   latecomers 46
   looking at 17, 18, 32–3
   and nervousness 59–61

proximity to 44–6, 47
relating to 17, 38
requests for action from 16–17, 23
silence of 29
size of 59, 61
and SPS 7–8
tailoring message to 11
watching reactions 38, 39
WIIFM 7

bad news 85–6
blank, mind 22, 26
body language 35–9
   abroad 86
   of audience 37–8, 39
   congruence 35, 39
   and dealing with questions 65
   eye contact 32–3
   and media interview 73
   off-putting habits 35, 37, 39
   of speaker 35–7
   stance 33, 34, 38
Brabazon of Tara, Lord 41, 42
brevity *see* duration; overtime; timing
butterflies *see* nervousness

chairs 44–6, 47
checklist for speaking 89
city dinners 79
clichés 31
communication channels 29–34

components of presentations 22
computer graphics 52, 55
conclusion 22–3, 27
  pitfalls 89
  summarising 23
conferences 85, 87
confidence, lack of 57
  see also nervousness
courtesy see sincerity
credibility of speaker 43
  and content 44
  and media interview 71, 73
culture of audience 17, 47, 86

delivery 29–34
  channels 29
  and nervousness 57–61
  verbal 29, 31
  visual 29, 32–3
  vocal 29, 31–2
Disraeli, B. 41
distractions 44, 46
dress 38, 39, 46, 47
duration of speech 26, 41–2
  After Dinner speaking 77–9
  introducing other speakers 83
  media interview 73
  retirement speech 83
  votes of thanks 84
  see also timing

empathy with audience 44, 46
environment, physical 44–6, 47
evaluation of speech 89
expectations of audience 7, 31, 44
explanations to audience 38
  and visual aids 53
eye contact 32–3

facts
  and media interview 73
  opinions and 43–4, 46
fear see nervousness
finishing 22–3, 27, 89

flip charts 51, 52, 53
  see also visual aids
Forces, Loyal Toasts 84
foreign language 86
forgetting
  by audience 23
  by speaker 22
funny stories 34, 79, 80, 81

good news 86
Grade, Lord 49
grammar and syntax 31

habits, nervous 37
handouts, rules for 51
hands 33, 37
  and standing 33, 37
hostile audience 37
Hubbard, Frank 35
humour 34, 79, 80, 81, 87
  offensive 34
  rules for 89

immediacy 31
impromptu speaking 21
interests and concerns of audience
    17, 43
introducing other speakers 83
introduction 22, 26, 27
involving audience 16, 17, 31, 34

Jessel, Sir George 77
jewellery 37, 38

kinesics see body language
Kissinger, Henry 29

language
  foreign 86
  tailored to audience 11
  unpatronising 18, 65–6, 87
latecomers in audience 46
lectern 33, 37
looking at audience 17, 18, 32–3

looking at audience (*continued*)
 media interview 73
 and nervousness 60
 see also body language; eye
  contact
looking at notes 34
Loyal Toasts 84

main points 9, 21, 26
 and media interview 73, 74
media interview 71–5
 basic techniques 71–4
 positive attitude 73, 74
 pre-grilling 74, 75
 proactive stance 73
 specialist courses 71, 74
 and voice 73
mind, blank 22, 26
Mitford, Nancy 86
Mizner, Wilson 63
motivated sequence 25–6

need step 25
nervousness 57–61
 butterflies 57, 59
 looking at audience 60
 mind going blank 22, 26
 nervous habits 37
 rules for overcoming 59–60, 61
 showing 37, 38–9, 61
Newton, Howard W. 81
noise 44, 46
non-verbal communication *see* body
  language
notes 19–27
 looking at 34
 and nervousness 59
NVC *see* body language

objections, dealing with 67–9
OHPs 51, 52, 53
opinions and facts 43–4, 46
overhead projector 51, 52, 53
 see also visual aids

overseas speaking 86–9
overtime, going 43, 46, 79, 89

pace of voice 31, 34
pauses 31, 60
physical environment 44–6, 47
pitch of voice 31, 34
pitfalls 1, 3, 89
points, main 9, 21, 26
 and media interview 73, 74
power of voice 31, 34
preparation 19–27
 importance of 3, 9, 89
 introduction, body and
  conclusion 22–3, 26
 main points 21, 26
 for questions and objections 63
 sources 21
 stages of 21–2, 26
 time necessary for 5, 9
 and visual aids 52
 see also conclusion; introduction;
  presentations; rehearsals;
  Specific Purpose Statement
presentations
 components of 22
 defined 3
 duration 26, 41–2
 After Dinner speaking 77, 79
 importance of 1
 motivated sequence 25–6
 purpose 5–9
 reasons for 7
 rehearsing 26, 27
 relevance to audience 11, 17
 retirement 81, 83
 team 54, 59, 85
 see also preparation
proposing toasts 79, 80
protocol 79–80
 Loyal Toasts 84

The Queen 84
questions, dealing with 63–9

questions, dealing with *continued*
  defining 66
  golden rules 67
  'I don't know' 67, 69
  importance of 63, 69
  listening to 65, 66, 69
  loaded 68
  media interview 73, 74
  preparation for 63, 69
  stages of 65–7, 69
  stupid 65–6, 69
  timing sessions 65
  treatment of questioners 65–6,
    68, 69
questions, rhetorical 16
quotations, using 23, 31, 79

regimental dinners 79–80
rehearsals 26, 27
  After Dinner speaking 77
  media interview 74, 75
  and nervousness 59, 61
  and visual aids 54, 55
  see also preparation
relevance of message 11, 17, 43, 46
repetition 23
retirement presentations 81, 83
reunion dinners 79–80
rhetorical questions 16
Roosevelt, Eleanor 57

satisfaction step 25
seating arrangements 44–6, 47
seminars 85, 87
sentences
  first and last 22, 23, 27
  length 31
silence
  of audience 29
  of speaker 31, 51
    and media interview 74
    and visual aids 51
sincerity and special occasions 79,
  81, 84, 87

slides 51, 52, 53
small audiences 59, 61
special occasions 81–7
Specific Purpose Statement 5, 7, 41,
  89
  achievable 8, 9
  and answering questions 68, 69
  preparation guidelines 7–9, 21
  specific contents 5, 7, 9
speed of speaking 26, 32, 34
  and nervousness 60
standing
  and hands 33, 37
  how to 33, 34, 38
  proximity to audience 44–6, 47
  and visual aids 44, 55
stories, funny 34, 79, 80, 81
subject of speech *see* topic
summarising 23
syntax and grammar 31

team presentations 54, 59, 85
television interviews 71, 73–5
  see also media interview
temperature 44, 47
timing 41–3
  After Dinner speaking 77, 79
  conferences and seminars 85, 87
  duration of speech 41–2
  and nervousness 60
  time necessary for preparation 5,
    9
  of visual aids 52
toasts, proposing 79, 80
topic 19
  credibility of content 44
  knowledge of 33
Trollope, Anthony 11

ventilation 44
verbal delivery 29, 31
verbal flagging 16
verbal paragraphing 16
visual aids 49–55

visual aids (*continued*)
  breakdown of 53–4
  computer graphics 52, 55
  effective 49, 51
  flip charts 51, 52, 53
  handouts 51
  OHPs 51, 52, 53
  pitfalls 89
  position of speaker 44, 55
  and rehearsal 54, 55
  rules for 49, 51, 52–4, 55
  slides 51, 52, 53

timing of 52
types of 51–2
use of pointer 53
value of 52, 54
visibility of 44, 55
visual delivery 29, 32–3
visualisation step 25
voice 89
  delivery 29, 31–2
  and media interview 73
  pace, pitch and power 31, 34
votes of thanks 83–4